SCIENCE ON THE EDGE

NANOTECHNOLOGY

WRITTEN BY
DIANNE MADDOX

BLACKBIRCH PRESS
An imprint of Thomson Gale, a part of The Thomson Corporation

THOMSON
GALE

Detroit • New York • San Francisco • San Diego • New Haven, Conn. • Waterville, Maine • London • Munich

For more information, contact
Blackbirch Press
27500 Drake Rd.
Farmington Hills, MI 48331-3535
Or you can visit our Internet site at http://www.gale.com

Photo credits: Cover: A. Yazdani & D.J. Hornbaker/Photo Researchers, Inc.; 20th Century Fox/The Kobal Collection, 40; © Bettmann/CORBIS, 11, 24; © CORBIS, 10, 15; © Tim Graham/SYGMA/CORBIS, 8; PeterHarris/Photo Researchers, Inc., 25; Roger Harris/Photo Researchers, Inc., 35; © Hulton/Archive by Getty Images, 12; Russell Kightley/Photo Researchers, Inc., 7; James King-Holmes/Photo Researchers, Inc., 26; Moredun Animal Health Ltd./Photo Researchers, Inc., 22; NASA/Photo Researchers, Inc., 37; Susumu Nishinaga/Photo Researchers, Inc., 30; David Parker/Photo Researchers, Inc., 17; Alfred Pasieka/Photo Researchers, Inc., 31; PhotoDisc, 21, 38; Photo Researchers, Inc., 6; Photos.com, 23, 28; © Reuters/CORBIS, 39; © Masahiro Sana/CORBIS, 41; Volker Steger/Photo Researchers, Inc., 19; Andrew Syred/Photo Researchers, Inc., 4; Victor Habbick Visions/Photo Researchers, Inc., 20, 32, 33; VVG/Photo Researchers, Inc., 36; © Tom Wagner/SABA/CORBIS, 13

LIBRARY OF CONGRESS CATALOGING-IN-PUBLICATION DATA

Maddox, Dianne, 1952–
  Nanotechnology / by Dianne Maddox.
    p. cm. — (Science on the edge)
  Includes bibliographical references and index.
  ISBN 1-4103-0530-9 (hardcover : alk. paper)
  1. Nanotechnology—Juvenile literature. I. Title. II. Series.

  T174.7.M33 2005
  620'.5—dc22   2004020047

Printed in the United States of America
10 9 8 7 6 5 4 3 2 1

TABLE OF CONTENTS

INTRODUCTION

THE NEXT SMALL THING

Throughout history, scientists have made big breakthroughs and big discoveries. These days, some of the biggest breakthroughs and discoveries are extremely small. They are being made in the exciting new field of nanotechnology. Scientists and engineers who study nanotechnology are trying to build devices that are as small as possible. The next big thing in science will likely be very small indeed.

An ant holds a computer microchip in this magnified image, illustrating the smallness of nanotechnology.

The roots of nanotechnology began over two thousand years ago when toymakers in China were making mechanical toys with very tiny moving parts. This delighted children, but it also inspired artisans to apply those skills in more practical ways. Over time, engineers, scientists, and artisans have worked to make machines—from clocks to computers—smaller and smaller. Now scientists are trying to make machines so small they can be seen only through powerful microscopes.

A scientist from Tokyo named Norio Taniguchi first used the term *nanotechnology* in 1974. He used it to talk about the work being done with the tiniest forms of matter: atoms and molecules. Nanotechnologists are engineers and scientists from all science disciplines, including biology, chemistry, and physics. They dream of being able to store the Library of Congress on something the size of a sugar cube, or of making a material that is ten times stronger than steel but lighter than a feather. These achievements may come about one day through new discoveries in nanotechnology.

CHAPTER 1

THINKING SMALL

The world that nanotechnologists study is incredibly small. In 1926, a man used a diamond point to write the Lord's Prayer on a piece of glass that was just 0.0016 inch by 0.0008 inch (0.04 millimeter by 0.02 millimeter). In 1983, a Japanese man wrote the names of forty-four countries on a single grain of rice. While these achievements may seem unbelievably small, the work in nanotechnology is on a much, much smaller scale.

Microorganisms like these bacteria live in a world that can only be seen through a microscope.

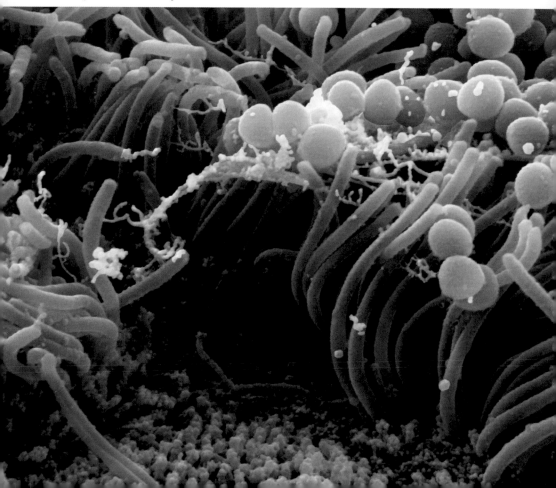

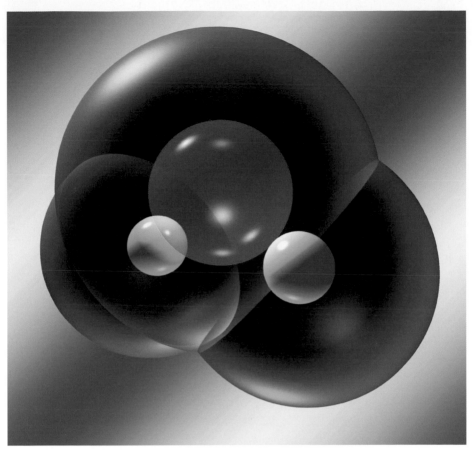

An illustration shows a water molecule and its one oxygen and two hydrogen atoms. Nanotechnology's challenge is to work at the molecular level.

To understand just how small things are in nanotechnology, it helps to compare some of the different worlds that scientists study. The world where people live and work, the macro world, can be seen with the naked eye. It can be measured in feet and miles or meters and kilometers. A thousand times smaller than the human world is the world inhabited by insects. It can be measured in inches or centimeters and millimeters.

Another thousand times smaller is a world that can be seen only through a microscope. The inhabitants of this microscopic world are microorganisms such as bacteria. This world can be measured in microns, or micrometers, which are 1 millionth of a meter.

Clocks had to be large before clock makers developed the mainspring, an invention that led to the wristwatch.

A thousand times smaller yet is the world that is studied in nanotechnology. In it, the inhabitants range from viruses down to the basic building blocks of matter known as atoms and molecules. Its unit of measure is the nanometer, which is 1 billionth of a meter.

A molecule is the smallest piece of a substance that can exist without breaking down the substance into the chemical elements that it is composed of. Each element is made of one kind of atom, and atoms combine chemically to form molecules. Water, for example, is sometimes called H_2O because the atoms that make up a water molecule are two hydrogen atoms (H_2) and one oxygen atom (O). Molecules are so small that one drop of water contains millions of molecules. The challenge of nanotechnology is to work at this molecular level.

The measurement that scientists use in nanotechnology is the nanometer. Nano is a prefix that means "billionth." A nanosecond is 1 billionth of a second. A nanometer (nm) is 1 billionth of a meter (0.000000001 meter), or one thousand times smaller than a micrometer. A nanometer is a measure so small that it takes about 40,000 nanometers to equal the width of a human hair.

The technology that enables scientists and engineers to work on the nanometer scale has developed over many centuries. Machines that were once very large have been made smaller and smaller. Clocks, for example, originally had to be big because large weights were needed to move the clock's parts and keep time. Later, clock makers invented the mainspring, a coil of wire that could be wound up and then would gradually unwind to move the clock's inner parts. It was this invention that eventually led to the development of the wristwatch.

Another example of a machine that was originally very large is a computer. Computers, as well as other electronic devices such as radios and televisions, need controlled electric signals to be able to operate. In the early 1900s, scientists invented a vacuum tube as a

A worker installs panels on an early computer. Early computers were large because they required vacuum tubes to operate.

way to control the flow of electricity. When they were first invented, radios, televisions, and computers all contained vacuum tubes, which were big and bulky. Early computers were big enough to fill an entire room, because they required so many vacuum tubes.

In 1947, three American scientists invented a device, called a transistor, that could take the place of a vacuum tube. A transistor is a tiny block with three or more electrodes attached. Like a vacuum tube, it controls electric signals, but it is solid and much smaller. As a result, computers, televisions, and radios made with transistors quickly became smaller in size and more portable.

A woman inspects a transistor, an invention that allowed computers, televisions, and radios to be made smaller.

A VISIONARY: RICHARD FEYNMAN

Richard Feynman (1918–1988) was born in Brooklyn, New York. Even as a child he was interested in science and in solving puzzles. When he was in school, instead of learning trigonometry from a book, he worked to figure out all the formulas himself.

Richard Feynman developed quantum electrodynamics, a new theory of physics.

Feynman graduated with a degree in physics from the Massachusetts Institute of Technology (MIT) in 1939 and received his PhD from Princeton in 1942. He worked with other scientists on the atomic bomb at Los Alamos, New Mexico, during World War II. After the war, he spent most of his working life teaching physics at the California Institute of Technology (Cal Tech). He loved teaching and felt that it gave him his greatest sense of achievement.

He developed a new quantum theory (quantum electrodynamics) and was awarded the Nobel Prize in Physics in 1965 along with two other scientists. In 1986, Feynman was appointed to the committee to investigate the space shuttle *Challenger* disaster. He researched it independently and was able to identify the cause of the explosion.

Feynman was perhaps the most famous scientist of his time. He was admired for his wit, his independence, and his curious nature. He saw most things in life as a puzzle waiting to be solved.

In a speech to the National Science Teachers Association in 1966, he said, "You can know the name of a bird in all the languages of the world, but when you're finished, you'll know absolutely nothing whatever about the bird. . . . So let's look at the bird and see what it's doing—that's what counts. I learned very early the difference between knowing the name of something and knowing something."

THE BIRTH OF NANOTECHNOLOGY

In this quest to make machines and their parts smaller and smaller, new ideas began to take shape. One of the foremost visionaries was Richard Feynman, an American physicist. Most scientists date the beginning of nanotechnology to a speech titled "There's Plenty of Room at the Bottom" that Feynman made in 1959 to the American Physical Society. In the speech, Feynman suggested that it would be possible someday to build structures atom by atom. He said, "What would happen if we could arrange atoms one by one, the way we want them?"[1] He envisioned that it would be possible to write the entire *Encyclopaedia Britannica* on the head of a pin. He also suggested that computers could be made smaller and faster and that tiny devices could travel within a person's body and correct certain medical problems.

Feynman even started things off by offering a one-thousand-dollar prize to the first person who could build a tiny working electric motor. His challenge was that the motor had to fit inside a cube with sides that measured just 1/64th of an inch (1/25th of a centimeter). To everyone's surprise, Feynman had to award the

Inventors have developed motors small enough to power tiny cars like this one.

prize just two and a half months later. William McLellan, a physicist from the University of California Institute of Science and Technology, made the tiny motor. He used a microscope, a toothpick, and watchmaker's tools to build it.

Since McLellan made his tiny motor, other motors have been made that are even smaller. In 1988, a team from the University of California made an electric motor that could be seen only through a microscope. The main spinning part of the motor measured just 60 micrometers in length. In 2003, an even smaller motor was made that measured just 200 nanometers across.

GETTING STARTED

Part of the challenge of making these microscopic machines is to be able to see them. Strong microscopes were needed for nanotechnology to be possible. In the 1930s, the electron microscope was invented. It was much more powerful than a regular optical microscope, which works with visible light rays. Electron microscopes use beams of electrons to magnify objects. Regular microscopes can magnify objects up to fifteen hundred times. Electron microscopes can magnify a specimen up to a million times. However, they were still not powerful enough to be able to show single atoms. Then in 1981, Swiss physicists Gerd Binning and Heinrich Rohrer invented the scanning tunneling microscope, for which they were awarded a Nobel Prize. This microscope allows users to see individual atoms.

The scanning tunneling microscope has a needle, or probe, made of tungsten. Using chemical and electrical processes, the needle is made so sharp that when an electrical charge is added, it will attract a single atom or small cluster of atoms. Scientists also found that besides attracting atoms, the needle could be used to move them around.

In 1989, scientists at International Business Machines (IBM) used the scanning tunneling microscope to experiment with this

A scientist looks into the eyepiece of an electron microscope. The microscope uses beams of electrons to magnify objects up to a million times.

capability. The scientists used atoms of xenon gas on a metal surface that was cooled down to $-452°F$ ($-269°C$). At that low temperature, the atoms were practically motionless. The scientists found that when they positioned the needle of the scanning tunneling microscope over an atom and applied a tiny electrical charge to the tip, the atom stuck to the needle. When they moved the needle to a different position, they decreased the charge and released the atom from the needle. Following this procedure, the scientists were able to spell the letters IBM using thirty-five xenon

COMPARING SIZES

1 meter = the width of a door
1 centimeter (1/100 of a meter) = the width of a crayon
1 millimeter (1/1,000 of a meter) = the thickness of a dime
1 micron, or micrometer (1/1,000,000 of a meter) = some bacteria
1 nanometer (1/1,000,000,000 of a meter) = the width of six carbon atoms

 1 inch = 25,400,000 nanometers
 a typewritten period = 500,000 nanometers
 the diameter of a red blood cell = about 7,000 nanometers
 a virus = 75 to 100 nanometers
 width of a DNA molecule = 2.5 nanometers

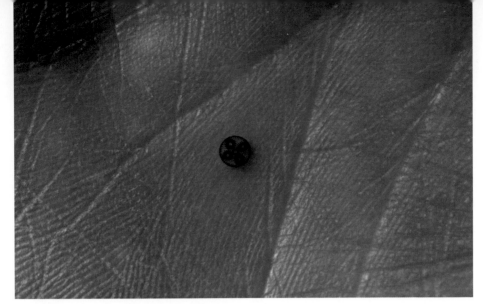

A close-up of a microgear on a person's hand illustrates the tiny size of nanotechnology machine parts.

atoms. This marked one small step in learning how to maneuver atoms successfully.

Interest in nanotechnology has grown dramatically since then. It received a big boost in 2000 when the U.S. government started the National Nanotechnology Initiative and pledged hundreds of millions of dollars for nanotechnology research and development. Nanotechnology research centers sprang up at more than thirty colleges and universities as well as at many private companies. Additionally, the United States is not the only country interested in nanotechnology. It has become an international endeavor.

The exact definition of nanotechnology is sometimes unclear. Some of what passes for nanotechnology is really work at the micrometer level. The National Science Foundation defines nanotechnology as working with materials and systems that have at least one dimension measuring no more than 100 nanometers, using processes that can control the physical or chemical characteristics of the molecular structures, and often, combining such structures into larger structures.

CHAPTER 2

NANOTECHNOLOGY TODAY

Products that make use of nanotechnology have been around for a long time. For example, tiny black carbon nanoparticles have been a part of tire manufacturing for years. The particles are only a few nanometers long and help keep the rubber flexible and strong. More recently, there have been products that contain other kinds of nanoparticles, such as sunscreens, stain-resistant fabrics, and certain cosmetics. What sets much of today's nanotechnology apart from earlier uses is the specific intent of using materials that are smaller than a micrometer.

TOP DOWN OR BOTTOM UP

Nanotechnologists generally fall into two groups. Some are interested in a top-down approach. They start with something larger and then try to figure out how to reduce it in size to nanoscale proportions. Others prefer to use a bottom-up approach. These scientists want to start with atoms and molecules and use them to build larger structures.

Some nanotechnologists who look at ways to make smaller computers or computer parts are using the top-down approach. The challenge of making electronic parts smaller and smaller has already come a long way. Transistors, which were invented to replace vacuum tubes, were made from semiconductor material. A semiconductor is a substance with special properties that allow an electric current to pass through it under certain conditions. The semiconductor material used most often is silicon.

Eventually, scientists decided that instead of making transistors one at a time, it would be more efficient to put as many transistors

A nanotechnologist works with laser beams. Some nanotechnologists use the top-down approach; others use the bottom-up approach.

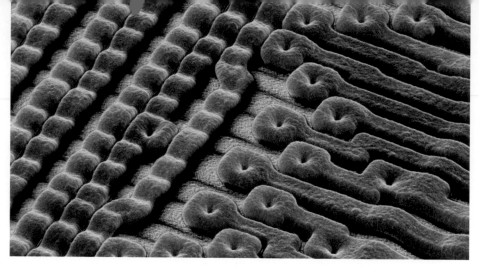
An electron microscope image shows the surface of a microchip. The most common process used to make microchips is photolithography.

as they could on one small piece of silicon. They put a group of transistors, called an integrated circuit, on a silicon chip. The first one was made in the United States in 1960. By 1975, over thirty thousand electronic components could be placed on one chip. Twenty years later, a single piece of silicon about .025 inch (6.3 millimeters) square could hold over 3 million components. Since the components were now of microscopic size, the chip became known as a microchip.

The process most commonly used to make microchips is called photolithography, a process very similar to photography. It starts with the creation of something like a photographic negative. This negative, called a mask or master, is a large pattern of all the circuitry to be put on the chip. Then the master is greatly reduced in size and the patterns are copied onto silicon chips.

Now nanotechnologists want to further reduce the size of microchips to create nanochips. Although photolithography could be used to make structures smaller than 100 nanometers, it would be very difficult and expensive. Therefore, researchers are experimenting with new processes and materials for making nanochips. These include using a scanning tunneling microscope to arrange nanoparticles into patterns and another procedure that uses a kind of stamp to imprint the patterns.

SELF-ASSEMBLY

Some nanotechnologists are interested in the bottom-up approach. This approach is not practical for producing the complicated patterns needed in electronics, but it can be useful in other ways. Part of this approach is based on the idea of self-assembly. These scientists look for their inspiration in nature, where many things are created through self-assembly. One example is a snowflake. A snowflake forms when dust particles are combined with cold temperatures and precipitation. Ice crystals form around the speck of dust and the result is a snowflake. Nanotechnologists believe that

Snowflakes and many other things in nature are created by self-assembly.

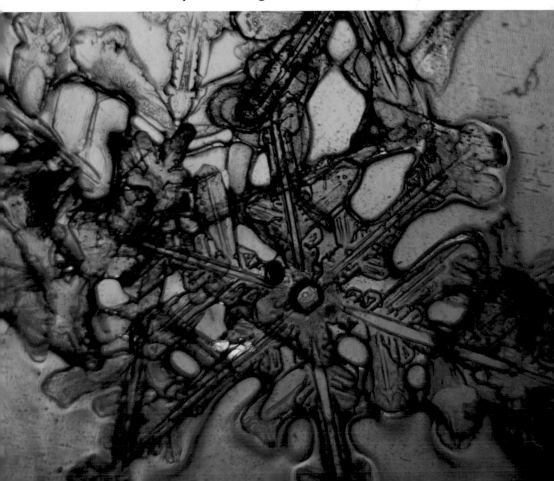

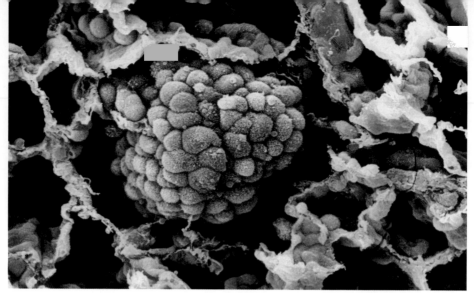

Doctors may soon find cancerous tumors like this one with Qdots.

with the right ingredients and under the right conditions, many things will be able to manufacture themselves, or self-assemble.

One nanomaterial that has already been created through a self-assembly process is called a quantum dot. Quantum dots, or Qdots, are semiconductor material crystals that consist of only a few hundred atoms. To make Qdots, scientists use chemical reactions that combine certain metal atoms with organic molecules. Qdots can emit tiny wavelengths of light in a variety of colors. Scientists are looking at ways to use Qdots to locate tumors. The Qdots could attach themselves to microscopic tumors and then, by radiating their lights, help doctors find the tumors. For doctors and patients, it would be extremely beneficial to locate and remove tumors at their earliest stages, when the tumors are quite small.

NEW MATERIALS

Another exciting outcome of current nanotechnology is the development of new materials. One key element that scientists are using in new ways is carbon, the chemical element C. Carbon is a main ingredient in all living things. When wood is burned, what is left of it is soot or charcoal, which is pure carbon. Other forms of pure carbon are graphite, which is what pencil lead is made of, and diamonds. The difference among these substances is the arrangement of the carbon atoms. In charcoal, the atoms are more or less disorganized. In graphite, the atoms form flat sheets. In a diamond, carbon atoms are bonded so tightly that they form one of the hardest materials on Earth. Carbon is important to nanotechnologists because it is plentiful and stable, and carbon atoms stick to just about anything, including other carbon atoms.

In 1985, Richard Smalley, a professor at Rice University in Texas, led a team of scientists who discovered a new form of carbon. Even though this kind of carbon molecule had been around

Carbon atoms bond to form a diamond, one of the hardest materials on Earth.

BUCKMINSTER FULLER AND THE GEODESIC DOME

The American architect and engineer R. Buckminster Fuller (1895–1983) had a dream of creating housing for people that would be strong and affordable. The dream led him to invent the geodesic dome in the 1940s. The structure of a geodesic dome is a network of connecting triangles that form half of a sphere. It is stronger, lighter, and

R. Buckminster Fuller invented the geodesic dome (background) in the 1940s.

more cost-efficient than conventional buildings. The geometric construction has the unique quality of increasing in strength and decreasing in weight the larger the structure is built.

Fuller's dream of people living in geodesic domes throughout our cities and neighborhoods has not come true. There are, however, thousands of geodesic dome structures around the world. One of the most famous is Spaceship Earth at Epcot Center in Walt Disney World in Florida. Although it is more fully a sphere than a dome, it is a great example of what geodesic construction is like.

since the beginning of time, it had never been recognized before. The molecule is an arrangement of carbon atoms into a shape like a little sphere. Formed from 60 carbon atoms (C_{60}), the sphere looks like a soccer ball. It also resembles a geodesic dome, a kind of geometric structure designed by American engineer R. Buckminster Fuller. Smalley and his fellow researchers named the carbon molecules buckminsterfullerenes in honor of Fuller. They are also known as either "fullerenes" or "buckyballs." The molecules are unique because they are hollow, very stable, and are able to withstand high temperatures and pressures. Smalley and his team were awarded the Nobel Prize in Chemistry in 1996 for their discovery. Moreover, scientists studying buckyballs have discovered other new forms of carbon molecules.

One of the most important new carbon structures was discovered in 1991 by a Japanese physicist. Instead of a sphere, he found a carbon molecule that formed a hollow cylinder. It looks like a long tube and is about 1 nanometer in width. He called it a carbon nanotube, or "buckytube." A nanotube has many special

An electron microscope image shows a nantotube, a carbon cylinder discovered in 1991 that measures about 1 nanometer across.

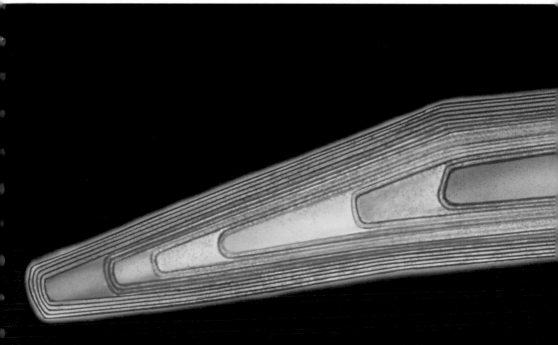

A chemist examines a molecular model of a nanotube. Nanotubes may someday be used to make new kinds of machines and materials.

properties. It is one hundred times stronger than steel, it can act like a semiconductor material, and is a good conductor of heat. This type of carbon has the greatest potential to build things that are stronger, bigger, and safer than ever before. A cable made of buckytubes just 0.08 inch (2 millimeters) wide, or the width of a ballpoint pen refill, could support 20 tons of weight.

Scientists predict that nanotubes could be used to make things from microscopic robots to earthquake-resistant buildings. Other possible products are fabrics that will not tear, extremely thin automobile bodies, and impenetrable body armor for law enforcement officers. So far, scientists have been able to grow buckytubes only to lengths of about 100 micrometers. When they can grow them in much longer lengths, then scientists will be able to build new types of buildings, bridges, and aircraft.

EVERYDAY USES

Some new nanomaterials are actually composites, or combinations of nanoparticles with other materials. These composite materials generally fuse a plastic or polymer with inorganic nanoscale particles. The combinations make a new substance with unique properties.

One company has developed a nanocomposite material it calls "Air-D-Fence," because it acts like a barrier to keep air from leaking out. In 2002, a new kind of tennis ball was introduced, the Wilson Double-Core, which uses Air-D-Fence. Inside the tennis ball, nanoparticles are combined with rubber polymers to seal in the air. This keeps the ball bouncing at least twice as long as a conventional tennis ball.

In addition, a company in France is using nanotechnology to make stronger tennis rackets. Many rackets are made of graphite, a form of carbon. New tennis rackets combine graphite with carbon nanotubes. The result is a much stronger racquet that is still lightweight.

Scientists are developing carbon to create a new source of drinking water.

Another composite nanomaterial being studied will allow water in the air to condense into liquid. Scientists are developing a form of carbon that can absorb water vapor from the air, concentrate it, and then transform it into usable water. It would be able to accomplish this without the refrigeration normally required for condensation. One day this material could provide a convenient and energy-efficient way to obtain drinkable water where none is readily available.

Nanotechnologists today are discovering new materials and researching how to use them. It is a field of science still in the beginning stages of figuring out which projects are worthwhile to pursue and which are not. Like explorers of the past, nanotechnologists are exploring an unknown territory. They are distinguishing between what is possible and what is not.

CHAPTER 3

WHAT ARE THE POSSIBILITIES?

Many predictions are being made about how the world will be changed through nanotechnology. The Interagency Working Group on Nanotechnology reported in 1999 that "Nanoscience and technology have the potential to change the nature of almost every human-made object in the next century."[2]

In his speech "There's Plenty of Room at the Bottom," Richard Feynman mentioned that before making any progress, scientists would have to learn much more about the world of atoms and molecules. He said, "Atoms on a small scale behave like *nothing* on a large scale."[3] This minuscule world has captured our imagination in movies such as *Fantastic Voyage* and *Honey, I Shrunk the Kids*. However, the nanoworld is not merely our world in miniature. It is a completely different environment with a different set of rules.

Even at the insect level, the air is much thicker in relation to an insect's mass. For an insect, to breathe is more like swimming in water than breathing air as people do. At the micrometer or bacterial level everything is very jittery. At normal temperatures and pressure, an average molecule vibrates about 10 billion times per second. At the nanometer, or molecular level, things get even stranger. Besides the molecular vibration, boundaries are not very well defined. The structure of an atom is often pictured as similar to our solar system with the nucleus as the Sun and electrons as the planets orbiting around it. However, scientists now believe that electrons are more like a cloud surrounding the nucleus. That is part of the reason why nanotechnology is so exciting. The

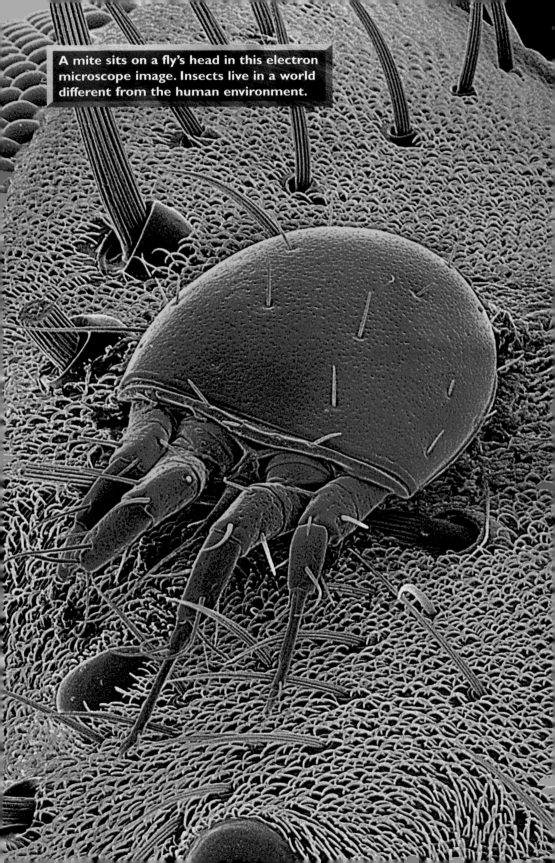

A mite sits on a fly's head in this electron microscope image. Insects live in a world different from the human environment.

field is so new and uncharted that scientists are discovering new characteristics about the nanoworld all the time.

Although a better understanding of how collective systems of molecules behave will be a prerequisite to assembling sophisticated structures, scientists are already dreaming of what might be. Feynman and others suggested that mastery of nanotechnology might one day lead to the invention of complicated molecular

Scientists must understand how molecules behave in order to assemble complex structures.

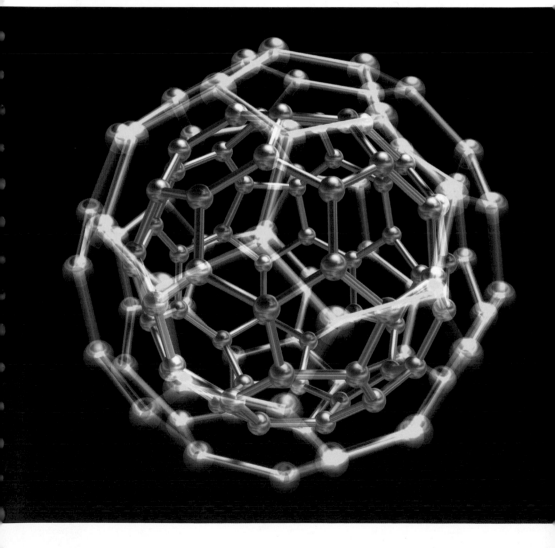

assemblies designed to perform particular functions. Sometimes such assemblies are referred to as nanobots for their small size and ability to perform complex robotic tasks.

A RADICAL VIEW

One controversial view of the future has been theorized by K. Eric Drexler. A graduate of the Massachusetts Institute of Technology (MIT), Drexler has helped popularize nanotechnology with his predictions. Drexler thinks that the biological forces that create so much of life on Earth can somehow be adapted to build nonliving objects. He calls this idea "molecular manufacturing," which means building things atom by atom, molecule by molecule. He first wrote an article about his theories and then published a book about them, titled *Engines of Creation*, in 1986.

Nanomachines may someday assemble large objects of all kinds.

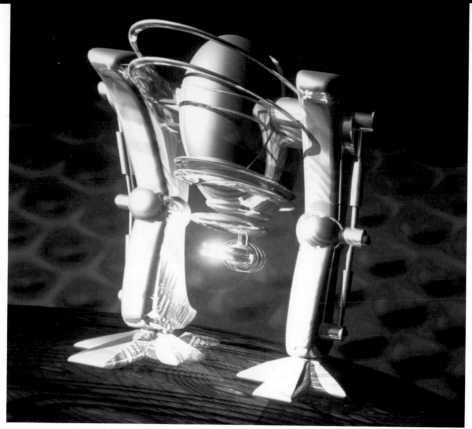
Nanobots like this one could make millions of copies of themselves.

Drexler envisions that for molecular manufacturing to take place, one must start with a microscopic machine called an assembler. The assembler would be able to put atoms in any kind of arrangement in order to build almost anything. However, since it would take millions of assemblers to make a large object, one key component of molecular manufacturing is the assemblers' ability to replicate, or make copies of themselves, in huge quantities.

In his book, Drexler describes how a rocket engine could be made using assemblers. He explains that self-replicating assemblers would be placed in a huge vat along with the plans for the engine, fuel for the assemblers, and the raw materials. First, the assemblers would multiply and then an army of them would construct the engine by combining the necessary molecules. The engine would be built in less than a day and without any human attention.

Moreover, the final product would be seamless, light, and strong—much different from today's engines, which are pieces of metal welded together.

In addition, Drexler theorizes that our everyday lives could be changed forever by these assemblers. He thinks that everything from dishes to carpet could be made self-cleaning. Anything people need could be created in the home, including fresh food such as meat, vegetables, and fruit.

However, many scientists have been critical of Drexler and his radical predictions. Richard Smalley said, "Self-replicating, mechanical nanobots are simply not possible in our world."[4] To answer some of his critics, Drexler published *Nanosystems* in 1992, which further explains his ideas about molecular manufacturing using nanosize assemblers. However, to date, no one has been able to make an assembler. When and if that happens, Drexler thinks his visions can become reality.

WET NANOTECH

Many predictions have been made in another area of nanotechnology by biomedical researchers. Their area of nanotechnology is sometimes called wet nanotech. They dream about using nanotechnology to diagnose medical problems and treat them. Research scientist Robert Freitas wrote Nanomedicine, a four-volume series explaining how nanotechnology might change the medical profession. He predicts that tiny nanobots might be injected into a person's bloodstream and travel throughout the body to detect and even repair problems. Freitas has theorized about a "respirocyte," which is an artificial red blood cell that can deliver oxygen in the body hundreds of times better than natural red blood cells. A respirocyte would help in the treatment of respiratory and cardiovascular diseases as well as strengthen a person's endurance or allow divers to hold their breath for hours.

A computer image shows a nanobot treating a diseased cell. Biomedical researchers hope to use nanotechnology to diagnose and treat medical problems.

The potential use of nanotechnology in medicine has already taken a step forward with the invention of an artificial organic molecule. In 1981, scientist Donald Tomalia invented a "dendrimer," which gets its name from the Greek word for "tree." It is shaped somewhat like an asterisk with branches that fan out in all directions and is about the same size as a protein molecule. Dendrimers have the shape and surface area to be well suited as a delivery system for medicine inside a person's body. The hope is that they can take the medicine to the part of the body where it will be most helpful. Researchers are also hoping that dendrimers will be used in gene therapy as a way to put healthy genes into cells that lack them. Other future nanomachines might be able to repair tissue, clean out cholesterol, destroy cancer cells, and fight a host of diseases.

LOOKING AT DIATOMS IN A NEW WAY

Diatoms are crystal-like, single-celled algae whose shape can look like a star or other item.

Certain organisms found in nature, called diatoms, have caught the attention of nanotechnologists. Diatoms are single-celled algae that exist every-where in water. They are at the bottom of the food chain but are important to photosynthesis and help create a quarter of the oxygen in our atmosphere. These tiny crystal-like structures are three-dimensional and have intricate geometric shapes that can resemble flowers, raindrops, stars, wheels, and many other items. There are an estimated 1 million kinds of diatoms and each one has a shell made of silica, the main ingredient in glass.

Scientists are studying diatoms for their potential to help build devices for the nanoworld. Mark Hildebrand, a professor of biology at Scripps Institution of Oceanography, said in the *San Diego Union-Tribune*,

The goal of nanotechnology is to synthesize incredibly tiny structures that can be used for all sorts of things in medicine, research, engineering and industry. But we're never going to be able to build structures like diatoms in a test tube, at least not anytime soon, so why not find ways to use or make diatoms that will do what we want them to do on the nano-scale?

It is already possible to grow diatoms quickly and cheaply. The hard part would be to grow them in just the right shape.

GOING UP: AN ELEVATOR TO OUTER SPACE

In the near future, however, materials made with the new carbon nanoparticles hold the greatest promise for creating structures that are stronger than ever before. Some researchers are proposing something entirely new made with carbon nanotubes: an elevator into space. Currently, it takes a great deal of rocket power to

An illustration shows NASA's proposed space elevator, a transport to outer space made with carbon nanotubes.

The space shuttle lifts off from its launchpad. The space elevator may one day end the need for expensive rocket fuel.

launch a spacecraft above Earth's atmosphere. If the spacecraft could be lifted 22,000 miles (36,000 kilometers) and then released into space, it would save energy and fuel. This is the dream of the National Aeronautics and Space Administration (NASA).

NASA has begun designing an elevator, or tower, that reaches into space. It would be anchored securely somewhere near the equator. The equator would be the best location: It does not have high winds, and a satellite could remain in a fixed orbit over the site. A tall base tower would be built and a very strong cable made of carbon nanotubes could connect the tower with the satellite. The spacecraft could travel up the cable and then be released into outer space. The discovery of carbon nanotubes has made this dream a possibility. Of course, the tower would be very expensive to build but could eventually save money, because expensive rocket fuel would not have to be used to launch spacecraft.

Military officers wear impenetrable body armor that may become standard uniforms for combat in the future.

WHEN SCIENCE FICTION BECOMES REALITY

Miniaturized people and their submarine traveled through a scientist's bloodstream in the science fiction film *Fantastic Voyage*.

In 1966, a movie titled *Fantastic Voyage* was released as a science-fiction thriller. The movie takes place during the Cold War, and both sides have developed a process of miniaturization that reduces people and objects to the size of a molecule. However, the process lasts for only one hour. Then a scientist discovers a way to eliminate the time limit, and while on his way to reveal this discovery to the United States, he is nearly assassinated. He suffers a life-threatening blood clot in his brain. To save him, five people in a submarine are miniaturized and injected into the scientist so they can travel through his bloodstream and destroy the clot with a laser beam. Since the miniaturization is possible for only an hour, the action in the movie is a race against the clock as well as a battle with white blood cells and other antibodies in the scientist's bloodstream.

In real life, this kind of miniaturization may never be possible. However, the designing of nanodevices and medicines that can travel through someone's bloodstream and make repairs is a major goal of medical research.

WHAT ARE THE RISKS?

As interest in nanotechnology is booming, so are the questions about safety and risks involved with new inventions. A key element of the bottom-up approach to nanotechnology is self-assembly. Some worry that once molecules begin to assemble or reproduce themselves, they may not be able to stop. This threat is known as "gray goo." While they might not actually be gray or gooey, tiny replicating beings that are invisible to the human eye and multiplying out of control could be disastrous. Some fear that they could overtake and destroy Earth's environment.

Moreover, as with chemical and biological weapons, microscopic or submicroscopic organisms can be very dangerous. They can cause illness or death in humans and animals. They can contaminate water and food supplies. There are also concerns about the consequences of medical treatments. If something were to go wrong with a nanosize device inside a human body, it might be impossible to find it and take it out.

From building materials to computers and beyond, nanotechnology will bring big changes in the future.

NANOTECHNOLOGY BREAKTHROUGHS

The future will bring many changes in our lives through nanotechnology. Computers will probably become smaller and more powerful. Buildings and bridges will likely be constructed of new, stronger materials. Doctors will have new methods to treat patients through better medical tests and new ways to deliver medicine.

Many people wonder when some of these achievements might become reality. While nanotechnologists have already made some new discoveries, scientists predict that major breakthroughs are at least ten, twenty, or even forty years away. There is no doubt, however, that big changes are coming, and that they will be very small.

NOTES

Chapter 1: Thinking Small

1. Richard Feynman, "There's Plenty of Room at the Bottom," speech to American Physical Society, December 29, 1959.www.zyvex.com/nanotech/feynman.html.

Chapter 3: What Are the Possibilities?

2. Interagency Working Group on Nanotechnology, *Nanotechnology Research Directions: IWGN Workshop Report*, September 1999, p. viii.www.wtec. org/loyola/nano/IWGN.Research.Directions.
3. Feynman, "There's Plenty of Room at the Bottom."
4. Richard Smalley, "Of Chemistry, Love and Nanobots," *Scientific American*, September 2001, p. 77.

GLOSSARY

atom: A tiny particle that makes up an element. Examples of elements are oxygen, hydrogen, and carbon.

buckminsterfullerene: A molecule consisting of sixty carbon atoms (C_{60}) arranged like a sphere. It is named after Buckminster Fuller, an American engineer.

buckyball: Another name for a buckminsterfullerene.

carbon: An element (C) that is plentiful in nature and essential to life.

carbon nanotube or buckytube: An arrangement of carbon atoms into a hollow cylinder.

dendrimer: A large synthetic molecule that is shaped like an asterisk.

diatom: A microscopic kind of algae that has a cell wall made of silica.

micrometer (or micron): A measurement that is 1 millionth of a meter.

molecule: A group of atoms that combine to form matter.

nano: A prefix that means 1 billionth.

nanometer: A measurement that is 1 billionth of a meter.

nanotechnology: The science concerned with structures that have at least one dimension measuring 100 nanometers or less.

quantum dot (Qdot): A semiconductor nanocrystal that radiates a light in different colors.

scanning tunneling microscope: A kind of microscope that allows a person to see and manipulate individual atoms.

self-assembly: The ability of natural substances to create themselves under the right conditions.

FOR FURTHER INFORMATION

Books

William Illsey Atkinson, *Nanocosm*. New York: American Management
   Association, 2003.

David Darling, *Micromachines and Nanotechnology*. Parsippany, NJ: Dillon, 1995.

Web Sites

Buckyball.com (www.buckyball.com). Information about buckyballs and other
information about nanotechnology.

How Stuff Works (www.howstuffworks.com). Information about science topics
including nanotechnology, atoms, and scanning tunneling microscopes.

Nanokids (www.nanokids.rice.edu). A Web site devoted to nanotechnology
education.

Nanotechnology Now (www.nanotech-now.com). Current information about
developments in nanotechnology.

Small Times (www.smalltimes.com). Information about new inventions in
nanotechnology.

Internet Source

Richard Feynman, "There's Plenty of Room at the Bottom," December 29, 1959.
www.zyvex.com/nanotech/feynman.html.

INDEX

ABOUT THE AUTHOR

Dianne Maddox is a freelance writer who lives in Oklahoma City.